MAZE

HUGH THOMAS

MAZE

HUGH THOMAS

Invisible Publishing

Halifax & Picton

Library and Archives Canada Cataloguing in Publication

Title: Maze / Hugh Thomas

Names: Thomas, Hugh, 1973- author.

Description: Poems.

Identifiers:
Canadiana (print) 20190085290 | Canadiana (ebook) 20190085304
ISBN 9781988784274 (softcover) | ISBN 9781988784335 (HTML)

Classification: LCC PS8639.H5738 M39 20019 | DDC C811/.6—dc23

Edited by Leigh Nash
Cover and interior design by Megan Fildes | Typeset in Laurentian
With thanks to type designer Rod McDonald

Printed and bound in Canada

Invisible Publishing | Halifax & Picton
www.invisiblepublishing.com

We acknowledge the support of the Canada Council for the Arts and the Ontario Arts Council.

Canada Council
for the Arts
Conseil des Arts
du Canada

ONTARIO ARTS COUNCIL
CONSEIL DES ARTS DE L'ONTARIO
an Ontario government agency
un organisme du gouvernement de l'Ontario

Lack of Communication

The solution is, as usual, dynamite.
You hand me the match, shooting cartoon sparks.
I light the fuse. Bang!
An explosion of confetti,
the sparkling remains of words we thought we knew,
marries us until we hit the ground

which, strangely, we never do;
suspension of disbelief supports us
further and further into Saturday morning.

Pantoum

Once again, poem becomes pantoum.
Everything repeats, even the moment of indecision.
Following its own footsteps, the picayune detail
reflected in a hundred mirrors
becomes part of the grand design

that you didn't even know about until
someone came to the door selling encyclopedias,
and told you about progress,
about the course of the twentieth century.

You don't believe him, never did
for an instant, but you think of him sometimes,
when sweeping the hard-to-reach corner of the stairwell,
all that stuff about planets,
and walking on the moon,
how long it takes to fall.

The Guitarist

It's useless to call her.
Laura monotonous,
Laura like water,
Laura like the wind
over Nevada.

Laura for distant causes.
Arena of the South calling her,
paid in white camellias.
Oh, guitarist!
Heart badly buried
by five shovels.

Bastille Day

In Paris, crossing this bridge with you
and many other people over hundreds of years.
Fireworks appear in the night sky:
that great Bastille in the clouds is being stormed again,
the Marquis de Sade free to walk among the living
until dawn. He is charming and French,
he loves the young men
who throw firecrackers at each other's feet.
You go off arm in arm with him.

Now you will have to walk all the way
    to Moscow with Napoleon.
By the time you arrive it will be mid-winter,
the army starving, the mountains impassible.
I send you messengers who get lost in the snow
that covers all the blank places on the maps.
I fold paper airplanes. What were they called
before airplanes existed?
I'll have to ask you when you crawl into bed, late,
smelling of mud and gunpowder.

Swedish Disquiet

The coming and going of yesterday
into the day before yesterday,
of yesterday into tomorrow—
it's confusing. Sometimes I worry
about waking up in the wrong country,
speaking Swedish to everyone—
only, actually, it's Norwegian.
When in a dream, speak the language of the dream.
Finland is a favourable business proposition.
Sweden is a rocky country on the Scandinavian peninsula
inhabited by figments of your imagination,
each of whom represents a fish.
Denmark—actually, I forget Denmark.
Anyway, this isn't what I wanted to tell you about.
I wanted to tell you about Africa,
but your cheeks are pale, my beloved,
and the cold fog envelops us once again.

Mutation

for Elizabeth Brandt

Eventually, the mutation becomes the norm.
More people go to the art gallery,
and the art gallery develops extra limbs.
At this point, micro-evolution takes over.
Individual works of art change
as layers of meaning are added or subtracted.
Prices in the café rise,
and a new waitress is employed part-time.
She sits at the till, does her biology reading,
watches the patrons adapt.

Roman Elegy

You dug me out of the ground,
    and I hadn't an idea in my head.
Love takes many forms: you might yowl
    over my torn-out heart,
or sleepwalk through a wall of knives to find me,
    or call me when you didn't mean to.
In the age of heroes, at 9:23 pm on Tuesday,
    one thing led to another.
The moon is waiting for a kiss,
    but she won't wait all night.
Did you mistake the goddess of love
      for the shadow of a snake
    disappearing into the crabgrass?
A young girl walking a tiger
    sold us water and we made libations.
The soldiers got on the train, all but the unwilling one—
    he had a drink on us, and Rome was
      queen of the world.

Opening the Dictionary

I.

good family, the King, ten crowns, evil, a ring
himself, his looks, chance, profit
white blossoms, tears
lack of curiosity
bake cakes, undress, clear the table
break in two, go to sleep

II.

milk, light, book, loaf
the main thing
near, first, alone
as he works
suddenly, absolutely, quite simply

III.

to glance at, to blow a kiss
to spend the night
to afflict, to throw out
to accuse, to speak ill of
to hanker after

IV.

memory, writing, works, friend
days, folly, portrait
tending to corrupt, suitable, full

there were a lot of people in the streets today

V.

to whine, to whimper
to squeak, to crinkle, to crunch
to twinkle, to shine
to take out, to utter, to publish
to hollow
to rummage in
to write, to be written
to wake up

VI.

pocket dictionary letter
bird ballad gadget
snowfall whisper

VII.

ink by force to talk to itself
engaged in reading
too, also, as well
and so am I

Mirror-writing

The window of the dark café is a mirror
in which the policeman directs traffic
towards the cannibal.
It is midnight backwards;
everyone is going away
to plug in their attachments.
They are trapped in the maze
in which we are also trapped,
but I am going to go to sleep,
and you are going to look at the moon.

Act of Thanking
for Erín Moure

Dictionary, notebook, courtesy.
This friendship a power blackout,
a knife sharpener by trade.
We are speaking/talking factory.

You ask. I ask.
How many? Song.
Understanding. (Not like a drainpipe!
Can't you hear it?)
In a song, spontaneous whoops.

Till later, wheelbarrow, road surface, far away.
Words, sea bird, diminutive.

TGV

I am dancing on a bridge
in Avignon. I have the plague
in an inside pocket.
Excuse me, I have to catch a train.
It is a train of great speed.
It is so fast it is invisible,
so fast that inside it, nobody moves.
The train tracks cover all of France,
and are being extended into the fourteenth century.
Soon, there will be no more waiting
for trains. The trains will find you
wherever you are.

Weekends

Walking around in my own hand-me-downs,
much too big. The dangling sleeves
knock the crystal glasses off the shelf.
Sit in the corner and be quiet!
Mummy is gone
but
here is a doll that says "Mummy,"
here is a blank diary
and an indelible marker that soaks through
one page to the next, to the next.
Didn't you follow the instructions?
Always turning right will get you out of the maze
if you're in a maze, but what if you're downtown?
Turn right and left alternately
and you might reach the lakeshore before dark.

Recognition

You're that jazz musician,
that one that was on TV,
or you could have been.
Isn't that so?
Something has to be excluded
but now that you mention it
I don't know what.
Like tying a tie, you're much better off
if you don't think about it.
You could always try a different channel.

Hungarian Bookstore

I am in the Hungarian bookstore in Toronto,
in what seems to be the poetry section.
I take a book off the shelf
and approach the cashier, who addresses
    me in Hungarian.
I'm sorry, I say, I don't speak Hungarian.
Oh, she says. She points to the author's name
    on the front cover.
He is the national poet of Hungary.
She opens the book to the frontispiece.
You look a little like him.
There is a certain resemblance,
though the poet is dressed in
    mid-nineteenth-century garb.
He had a great soul, she continues.
No one knows what happened to him.
He could be living in Toronto.
Yes, I say, yes, I'll remember that.

Inscription for a Cast

You've discovered
a new way
of falling down stairs,
something we knew
we needed
but not how
much.

Coffee

Surely arranging to meet for coffee
would have been easier in the nineteenth century.

I would have a timepiece in my vest pocket.
We would meet either before or after church.

We would raise carrier pigeons, then exchange them.
I would write my message on a strip of paper

and fasten it about your pigeon's leg.
A few words would be more than enough.

Cento

Just go to the graveyard and ask around.

American Sonnet

America *mi amor*
proud to natural beauty
long may your smile take them all
#1 slouch empire

imagination emporium
ruffling your first lace
promptly remove shameless fur trim
you are missing out

my country for sure
God bless cutie pie
crybaby remember
kiss me broken

enjoy offering irregularities and variation
hydraulic dream-girl must-have America

Summer

In the evening the cuckoo's cry
in the woods ceases.
The stalks of wheat bend lower,
and also the red poppies.

Black storm clouds hang
above the hill.
The cricket's old song
dies away in the field.

The leaves of the chestnut
no longer stir.
Your dress rustles
against the curving stairs.

Silently the candle glows
in the dark room;
a silver hand
extinguished it;

windless night, without stars.

First Aid

Dampen slightly and apply gently to wound.
Check heart rate, and the time,
and how your hair looks reflected in that shard of glass.
It looks great! Loosen your tie
if you're wearing one. If not, put one on
before the knock at your door.
It's the police with a warrant,
or a delegation from the President,
never someone wanting your autograph
just because you are you.

I detail the verbal exchanges with the affronted voyager on distant terraces, each equivalent in the space of the citation. Attempt in the morning: the magnolia garden inspecting its blue lack. Through the telescope, beautiful women make jewellery and dissolve in water.

My senses cheated, I flew for justice to the grape-sellers. Sally, in the palace of the oldest garden shed, high on the scale of perfidy, spread me with mayonnaise and red peppers.

Nell had gone into the discotheque, and I did not wish to interrogate the rest of the philosophers. I compared myself to the alphabet and knew I was getting younger. Down the street, a pope's skeleton worshipped a novel of smoke.

"Do the birds know?" It was a time of infantile enjoyments, glasses, high jump, sidewalks. The philosopher sat on a bag of money. He dissed me. His cape made of books and feathers was an imaginary ending that closed around me. Only Laura or Sara could rescue me from this language attendant.

Enough time sent me knights on horseback with chocolate-covered strawberries, and I was overwhelmed by a fear of intimacy. In this city you must wash your hands before eating, persuaded by the bells from the mountains, selling a new day and its fruits. A strange rover knows many fine things and follows his premonitions to the most capricious sales.

When my animal trembles to music, he is buried in cement; the sleepwalkers swim above him. Through the narrow glass, the young man in leather wants to alight, but he must flutter near the crow's nest to be lassoed by a passing knave. Will it happen in May? There is no language without disappointment.

Cross Traffic

Does not stop.

Bath

When I
am in the bath
it is always *my* bath
that I am in.

I sink deeper
into the tub.
All around me
the water rises.

I pull out the plug
and the water
runs down
the drain.

I shiver
in the cold air.
I have not yet
invented towels.

The Straw Dog-Man

He speaks clearly but no one understands him.
He is brightly painted.
He dislikes lists.
He has plentiful flowers but no roots.
He has written books on popular psychology.
When he arrived in Europe, he changed his sex.
He is not a fond recollection of past time.
He believes all sexual relations to be adulterous.
He has difficulty describing everyday occurrences.
He is no one else's clever idea.
At the height of the festival, he will be thrown
    into the river
and the river will carry him away.

Metropolitan

The two sicknesses common in this epoch
   are heat and isolation.
Miracles are also part of the impermeable equipment.
The water is your family. The subway is culture.
Eat your ticket. Your future is our compromise.
Language is a door. At the door, we watch you turning
   out the lights.

Visible City

Farewell to the voyager—panorama—Atlantis—centre of the world—a written body—hammock—anchor— plunge!

The June hotels are on fire by the sea. Admire the authentic goldfish in the stranger's net. History, the city's poor aunt and mercenary love. The antique wind explodes in electric flute music. Imposters in a palace of mirrors hold on against the gale of arrival. The architect has begun his opera, a dictation that doesn't end. The doves' quarter tells diverting lies. Nostalgia is the splendour of velocity. The clock door closes behind you. On every street, the avant-garde industrializes. Your destination is an observatory of the world. Improbabilists produce the true. Decline the ambulance's invitation. Become rustic and affirmative.

Chicagoland

We zoom down the freeway.
A river runs alongside, lapping.
There is our hotel, flying on ahead of us,
glittering in the last sunshine,
an instance of the new kind of weather,
downloadable from the Internet.
A horn honks, and another:
a stochastic process predicting the stock market.
Soon, in a great squealing of tires,
we will arrive in the traffic jam
that is our final destination.

Some Swedish Poets

I. Chaise-loooong

I SHALL get dressed, my pyjamas are going blind

BOLster, thanks, animals, also men,
ungloomy eye-filters. Listen
in. You dickhead.

Say you are riding horseback, poet
GROAN with
out of sight
          CRUMpets

                    dream hair sets sail
                      in a salon to
                          Odessa
                              worldly bucket

II. Tiller

You fell over, then I fell over. Place of rest.
Snowflaking sleep melted. Summary.
Summery. Mountain birches are startling. Signs of
distraction. You think big. Man after my own
head (mountain) is a nut (mountain). You see
Fran who is swelling with thanks. Thanks for nothing.

III. Elf Daughter

I've had enough of the sea, but I remember the moon,
bathing in the wind and I'm sinking, oh,
    fish me out, thank you
I've been swallowed by a WHALE. Dear whale,
we could get on. I will stay below decks
in my midshipman's uniform. Mornings are long.
Afterwards, a joke and a little more.

Get your vile paws off me! (Go wash.) MOVING VAN
Beeeep! They have come for the birdcage.
    Bruising effort,
but they bear it away.

Pickle Factory

> *"I worked in that pickle factory. It didn't*
> *really close down."* – JENNIFER LOVEGROVE

I. It didn't really close down

It grew legs and set off down the road.
The sun shone, the birds sang,
the pickles were green and crisp.
Soon it would be time to pay
the debts of a dead man,
to count kisses with a princess.
For now, the road does all the work,
bringing far mountains nearer,
opening up the hills.
The pickle factory
moves its new legs up
and down, up and down.
Along the road,
it meets one scoundrel after another
and follows all their nonsensical instructions.
That is how it finds its way to the city.

II. I worked in that pickle factory

The delight I took
in dancing among the tear-stained vats
is no longer appreciated
by you, or anyone.
I am as irrelevant as an appendix,
and as angry. I feel myself swelling
with useless and toxic data:
trade figures, fatality rates.
Buried among them
my name you will never guess
not that you ever tried.

Sappho XXXI

Fun time at the movies
I'm an unknown erotic and anxious toy
iodine and plasticine explosion added
   so specific

and gelid as heroine into human
cardigan and lungs up to a thousand
scarred us, time broke as many
   loud and taken

a lack came in language, a subatomic
authentic chrome undead romance
up to see out enormous empire
   's acquired basis

a quiet address catch dreams
pay and agree, chlorate of poems
empathic, the old epidemic
   things themselves

all point to lament, epic and open to

We Get Lost

Understanding was like a dance on ice.
Sometimes we fell down and took
    a long time to get back up.
Our hands were small creatures that followed us.
We lit ourselves on fire in the snowy street.

It was an emergency winter.
Claire: with your freckles and empty eyes,
and the dog in your heart.

Romanian Poem
for Maria Erskine

This is one of my early poems,
my poems written in Romanian.
I write it in Romanian
because I am happy.
I write it for you.
I write it as one Romanian to another.

Safety Instructions

1. Crowd around the table. Watch out for the overhead fans. Only cabin personnel may sing into the microphones. Try out a few simple dance moves. Pile up your baggage and climb on top. The television will tell you what to do.

2. The small dog waiting outside the door will bark twice. Put on your hat. Turn your tray table sideways. Look out the window or you will be decapitated. Wave to the passengers left inside.

3. Stay flexible and keep smoking your pipe. If you have no pipe, one will be supplied by the cabin crew. You can use your pipe to blow bubbles once you are a safe distance away from the wing area.

4. Jump onto the slide. Look for the pine tree that grows out of the cliff. Ignore the TV antennas appearing everywhere. Put your heads together. You might find love or a buried treasure. Come on, jump onto the slide. I can't keep talking like this forever.

5. The smoke is very thick, but I think I see doors ahead. I already told you all of this.

6. Rest seduced at the back of the plane and wait for yourself. The equipment will initiate you into the spark.

The Capital of Azerbaijan

Yesterday, two crows watched
from the tree outside my window.
Today, the tree has flown away.
What comes before "One for sorrow"?
Today, I have to answer my own questions.
My glasses are on the coffee table beside the crossword.
The capital of Azerbaijan is A.

Juvenile Ode

In a long widow thirst stuck,
from Jordan's midst red and growing,
and with ivy crowned the impossible person's
  silver-armed trap.

Foot sparks tankless in swamp. A museum
  of natural history
flourishes in freedom. Like fish-flies
trees' crooked roots go out of tune and love
  scrambles away.

Horses' wild flight his late cup
fluttering out of the frost, as lying days
came in a crowd to bathe their clocks
  in the evening light.

Trodden by no one, the garden where a geyser
shot from the stone brook; and he knew
something forgotten under his innermost skin
  listing towards hope.

Stars

When night comes,
I stand on the steps and listen:
stars swarm in the garden
and I stand in the dark.
Listen, a star just fell with a clang!
Don't walk on the grass in bare feet;
my garden is full of shards.

The City

for Stuart Ross

Stone by stone we will rebuild the city.
We will begin with the sky.
In more and more houses, tea will be made.
Down more and more streets, buses will run.
We will continue the card games begun by others.
There will be a few trees,
a few scars, a few garage sales.
A church covered in Christmas lights.
The wind has trouble remembering,
but the phantom of the previous city
is engraved in the shadows. Yesterday,
this city was named Toronto,
and today, it will be named Toronto.

Turkish Letter

A misspelled letter heroically swum across your body of water conjures massive blackouts. We rehearse *Moby Dick* in translation, that of a million monkeys. We discover gunpowder and sodomy.

Prompter, I fix what needs to be broken. Like a lead pencil, editorial and blue, I compose a leader in the narrow margins of error.

A puppet sings opera in my tedious head. I promise to modernize the revolution, to train leaders in zombie opera tortures. Your albino voice propagates on the radio.

I know you've permuted leftover moonlight by the docks. I know puppets may or may not be the plague. I'm going to leave my i's undotted, cross my t's when I come to them, and find you in New York, amid the Egyptian gods, dead novelists, and angle-headed hipsters.

Exercise

As far as I know, this is an excellent exercise.

I take care not to destroy the editors' implicit permission.

"Permission" means enclosure, as around a garden.

I can easily imagine a single poem as my source.

The Hungarian word for apple is the same as
    the word I remembered.

It is of course clear that the sky needs to
    emerge into discourse.

A single tomato is far more interesting than
    dozens of others.

Every word I write is bound to narrate you somehow.

Music I Heard with You

Poverty-stricken Brahms and elegant Schubert,
in matching neckties, danced to a Chopin ballad

while the string quartet smoked
and looked worried (Beethoven, *adagia*).

And lazy Shostakovich, at 4:30 pm,
still in his underwear.

A choir in the clouds hummed a Bach cantata
while somewhere in the world someone was coughing

and Bach was galloping on horseback,
gazing into his crystal of disinterest.

The fierce demons pursuing him
suddenly just seemed wistful.

Respect for Mozart's *Requiem*
kept us from the piano

or we'd have sawed its legs off,
sold them for pocket money.

When I was with you, the ravens
and milktrucks made such music.

Self-portrait Unwilling to Sit

I broke the dressing-table mirror
by throwing rocks from a distance!
Dawn came in a thousand fragments
of a countryside too close to see
clearly. Minimalist and uncomfortable,
not much help in a crisis.
Hey, friend, wait up.
If it's a picnic you're rushing to, tell me,
what is its place in the historical process?
Biting into a peach, summer
was full of erudition.
Sirs, I know little about art,
but something about the sky.
The territory of truth
grows narrower and narrower;
science pushes it to one side.
Now the likeness begins to appear.
A moment made of porcelain,
a slushy smear,
a tramcar apocalypse
on the move, dragging behind
dissonance, divine regret,
a story that lengthens
in this century that never ends.

Epithalamion

Millennial and unlikely music
sees us two traditionally zapped
with a single exigency.
Faces glowing and necks bite-marked,
the rosy blossoming of the truthful mania
not the state emergency with police, but precisely
the daily waiting, the creases, the
    economy-size silverware,
the unpronounceable and nameless kisses.

The work of the mowers many approve soberly,
but unremarked, mostly unpaid, their names forgotten,
those who took off their pants in global porosity.
To forget these sojourners
misunderstands today's poetry
overgrown with wildflowers.
Poetry is a pagoda, built of friendly embracings,
like a square dance complicating society,
voyaging through better and worse, remaining new.

Today a ticket to days of radishes
and saliva, chosen days when skin spoke
in gestures unrecorded in any diary,
capable of bacterial smear, praise,
naked respect, exalted absence,
cherries wrestling with heaven,
a burning list we sit up late compiling,
seeking some colossal nothing. We might name it trust.

Welcome

How warm it is today!
Would you like a cigarette?
I have a letter I would like to send.
Wait for me.
Would you like to share morning coffee?
Where is the railway station?
I do not understand you because
    I do not speak Japanese.
This is a beautiful city.

Danish Lipogram

Outside Copenhagen, away from the lake,
you were hoping to meet someone,
but you can't think of his name.
You look into a sandwich shop, but they have no
    smoked fish,
no organic onions, and no bread. Also, no beer.
You consider going to the hairdresser's,
    but decide against it.
You will have to proceed north, south, or west,
always turning left,
going only on yellow, avoiding all doors.
The professional school can't help you;
the bus driver can't give you directions.
You might hear a zither,
or even a quiet xylophone, but not a flute.
This isn't a dream; there's no use
    trying to open your eyes.

Saga Heroine

for Elinor Thomas

I threaten to translate you into Icelandic.
You gurgle, undaunted.
A thousand years ago, I was speaking
    much the same language.
You, too, will become one of those ambiguous heroes.
You will grow to an enormous size,
and lift the stone that was waiting to be lifted.
You will discover America, call it something else.
When someone whose name won't be recorded
asks for a light, you just might burn down their house.

Night in a Coal Pit

How do you extricate yourself?
With a broken lever that connects to nothing?
By putting on a different face?
Someone puts the sun in a cage, gets angry about it.
Meanwhile, you have disappeared into the panorama.

Unofficial Translation
for Sarah Burgoyne

Only what freezes is called water.
Goodbye is a direction
to which dogs sing the best songs.

The Man in the Bear Suit

The man in the bear suit
isn't wearing a bear suit.
He is holding a piece of paper
with the word "bear" on it.
He smiles self-consciously
and bares his yellow teeth.
A bear at a poetry reading!
Imagine that.
The poet makes him do a headstand,
then try out some dance moves.
For the finale, she gives him a unicycle.
He has never ridden a unicycle before
but keeps his balance perfectly.
Then the poem is over.
The poet is very modest:
she directs some of the applause
to the bear. His friends shout themselves hoarse.
I knew then
I would have to write a poem
to commemorate these events
after I had completely forgotten them.

He Said

I. Landscape

A green light shines over the planet.
A yoga studio starts to grow in a vacant lot.
A man remembers a disease and a skyscraper.
The happy muses bury themselves in the road map.
The freshly washed hairdresser flaps in the breeze.
Maria flies in the open window.

II. Does Kevin Know?

I saw it on a T-shirt:
Zesty Cheese Doritos.
Drop everything.
No more questions.

III. Invasion

We break off the dictation
for a Viking invasion,
for a medicinal meal in company,
for a struggle with a book,
for a ride in an antique automobile,
for a date with an alien,
to take off these new legs,
to book a ride on a mold spore,
for a story about a noisy psychologist,

for a bird's tomb,
for a fern with nose hair,
for a hasty watermelon,
for a cigarette from my sister's pack,
for a flimsy waybill,
for simultaneous iodine,
for whatever helps,
for a good excuse,
for Anna, a poem.

IV. Ontario Vacation Pictures, Sorry

We climbed higher and higher
until we met a lake whose water was tilted.
That's where the world starts. (There's a plaque.)
Both of us and the lake climbed higher and higher
until we met another lake.

My father and I
exchanged eyesight.
A so-called breeze tousled
the lake's thin grey hair.

(Behind us,
the car was walking the gangplank
out over empty space.)

My father's laser beam shot my head.
"I think I'm gonna croak."
He put his foot over my heart
and started to jump
into the water.
"Take me to your planetary din."

Back in the car
we arranged a silence.
The radio commentators (closed-captioned)
said we had invented a new sport.

If we had devoured Paris
a hundred years ago,
the city might remember my father
swimming along its log-plank boulevards.

Now, my father
floats into the air.
Now, the car is inside me.
As we roll downhill backwards,
I get younger and younger.
When the egg timer goes off
I will have negative-one brothers.

When the snow falls off the mountain
I take a bite
and put it back.

V. Countable Angel on Coffee Break

I am a darling sprocket.
Look at me!

VI. Over Living

The window blows cold air at the palm trees.
The insurance policy dissolves under a thousand
   raindrops.
Millionaires the size of microbes crawl over my crops.
The sound of the ringing telephone is coming from
   the barometer.

VII. Tree in the Room

The room is sick.
Its leaves are yellowing.
Mother calls in the window.
The tree's hands are shaking.
I shake hands with the tree.
We are frightened, or else it is summer.
You can see a long way, except for the leaves.
Mother calls from below, she's very small,
and now she is turning to smoke
but her arm is still waving.
The machines chirp.

River the colour of her eyes,
too dark to swim in.
I hang on tight.
All the trees are here, she says.
I don't say it's enough.
In the distant corridor someone is pacing.

VIII. He Said

A Swedish citizen.
A beautiful eraser.
Down the shoe mine.

Linear C

for Leigh Nash

After this one is another one.

Cabinet Hopes

Were I Secretary of Education
I'd have graduating seniors across the nation
in teams of two roll dice,
take their chances:
who is the fairest?
In some midwestern town
beauty unrecognized among us.

But instead I am Postmaster General
of a post office that is metastasizing
in every human heart.
So much mail goes undelivered
and I must read all of it,
never finding your telltale
illegible handwriting.

Launch Party

When I arrive
the party is already in orbit.

Someone hands me a glass of wine
which hangs in mid-air,
as do these poems
when they are released from this book.

They shimmer like soap bubbles.
How lucky we are
to be part of this experiment.

We touch our foreheads together
so we can hear ourselves think.

"I think we just passed David McFadden
in a lawn chair, held
up by a hundred helium balloons."

Early

As through the curtain an unbelieved
morning shines   the beautiful
came early   not a thought in your head
to hold you back

not the almost deadly poems
not the cat with its silver glare
too cool for raspberries   you sleep
and only later the blue of your eyes

unnamed in the rose garden
what shone there
as might be held to the lips
already slightly singed

Girls Who Eat Flowers and Fail Their IQ Tests

We got used to the old questions
so they changed them.
The new IQ test is finding the room where the test is held.
Riding a bicycle improves your IQ.

Ten years, and they never change the streets.
What kind of maze is this?
Boredom is part of the new IQ test,
and also deciding if this shirt goes with these slacks.

I scored much better on the old questions.
First came a big E, then a T and an I,
and so on, smaller and smaller,
all the way to Q and Z, which score ten each.

They gave me glasses, which give me headaches,
so I take pills
with something written on them
that's too small to read.

My friend Megan
eats five kinds of edible flowers.
"They make me happier but hungrier," she says.
I think it ought to be legal.

Some people say marriage should only be
between a man and a woman,

not between a woman and a flower,
but I say, "Wherever there's love."

I say it to the driver of the Spadina streetcar.
He tells me there's one more westbound subway,
but none going east,
not anymore.

From the Time

The marble sky is broken.
I will arrive on the moon by boat.
I will arrive at the end of my bones.
I am indirectly on a quest.
When I can, I sort.
I experiment with water and its benefits.
I will repent of its vestiges.
I will salvage a greeting.
I am divided by a limit.
I feel all the accidental voltage of the ordinary.
I remain hopeful.

Fresh Morning

Coughing, because of the grass in the landscape.
Oh, my wooden leg!
It could explode
heartwarmingly.
This is no draft to be frightened of,
just a memory of the future,
the far distant future.

Triumph

What fraction I? A delve of endlessness
in everything's great act.
One whirled among millions,
a first star like some last release.
Triumph at life, of other, triumph at finish till!
That the moment ice-cold run its ardour,
hear night's deepest flood,
stand as mountain under sun.
Time changes, understands, controls:
you come with new ranks, a thousand lists to tie me.
Sun, fill my lungs with honey.
The stars are going slower,
and nonetheless very quietly.

Key of Roses

for Maria Erskine

Demobilized pigeons throng the park.
We wait for each other. We cross the pool,
raising barely a ripple.
A mythological animal
—you say griffin, I say narwhal—
stops us with an extended claw,
says something in Flemish about life and gardens.
The windows were illuminated even if we weren't,
and there was dancing among the chimneys.
Overhead, let down on a string from heaven,
a glockenspiel, as such a total disappointment!

The Strange Mine of Pork Poetry

I vaulted into the ruins, lost my skin for one or a dozen days. Sharp sticks poked me into the territory of poets who specified their street addresses. Not enough, those lectures of miasma given by a mime—I plugged myself into the electrical circuit, received an immediate shock.

The stratagem that sold me ruins offered drums and furniture, contact with poets leery of bestsellers, literary arms, or—sob!—restaurant meals. With them, I made examinations down the strange mine of pork poetry, grew wings, became curious about flowering shrubs.

Sometimes I would get a letter, then lose it on the garden path. The oldest of poems is a short life, like all our names. A poem written in vices, for an aunt, or the ghost of a bicycle, mesmerizing like an opera in falsetto, calms the troubles of other poets. The last revision is a glass of water, the poem's assault against the form of the book.

Twenty-three Plus Seven

The Lord is my sherbet; I shall not want.

He maketh me to lie down in green patches: he leadeth me beside the still water beetles.

He restoreth my sound: he leadeth me in the patholo-gies of right-of-way for his nana's salad.

Yea, though I walk through the valse of the shadow play of death duty, I will fear no evolution: for thou art with me; thy roe and thy stag they comfort me.

Thou preparest a tablemate before me in the presenti-ment of mine enfoeffments: thou anointest my header with oiler; my cup fungus runneth over.

Surely goof and meridian shall follow me all the day-dreamers of my life force: and I will dwell in the house-coat of the Lord for ever.

Swedish Winter

In the dark hotel of a barn:
a bed of dead stones.
Upstairs, the rusty winds.
Father pulls up in the loud dream-wagon.
Here the road becomes ice.
We turn away from the stones, the empty house.

Albanian Suite

I. Apple

So to say, never again
uneaten.

Someone gave me a bump on the head.

II. Parade in the Rain

Perhaps I was looking for some onlooker
but the rain was impenetrable.
Some kind of friend you are!

III. Triangle

Like you, I am practising at
being misunderstood.

IV. !

"Yes, yes,"
a knock at the door, then you find yourself illustrated

once you wake up the next afternoon.

V. Boy and River

I am not getting wet
because it hasn't occurred to me.

We loiter under the narrow umbrella
of the summer rain,

pass back and forth an unlit cigarette,
waiting for Prometheus.

VI. Reading Homer

Replace your head
with another one.

Then try on someone's hat—
maybe someone who's very unlucky.

Please ignore the perpetual performance.

VII. Ironclad

(Without exaggeration)
the clocks, their conspiracy
(from up close).

VIII. Going to Italy

I won't go to Italy whatever you say.
You mentioned vitamin shots and rugs,
cigarettes and sopranos. You're a pirate
with an epilogue. Chain your mouth shut,
it'll only get you into more trouble.
There is only one Colossus,
and I will find it. The dictates of the tiger
form a gigantic labyrinth. I am complaining
in advance. If I get out of this one alive, so help me,
I will buy my own sandwiches.
Some gushing liquid—was it time passing?—
there is a long-distance call on line one.
I'm so sorry to disappoint you,
    but I'd make a terrible Roman.
Like everything I told you, and everything you told me,
it's just a story.

One Size

Fits all.

Dream

This dream we sleep in is slated for demolition.
Sound travels slowly in this old house.
Feet travel faster. Hurry, hurry.
We must save the flashlights, the fire extinguishers,
the wax apple off the altar. We must save everything.
It will take just a minute, one minute after another.
After innumerable eons, I will meet you
    on the back deck.
We will count each other's heads.
When that day comes,
may we have no more than one each.

Contemplating Sunset at West Lake

Take down the fence or we will have to cry.
Surrounded by mountains, now I need a shave.
You, too, must get into the narrow boat.
Her face is all that is left.
After a long time, we go home and eat cake.
Happy birthday to someone.
A message can be extracted from the lake.
All the explanations must be saved for later,
when it is my turn to paddle and your turn
    to play the lute.
Do not take off your hat. We will have to
    sleep two to a bed.
It is beginning again at another table,
    provided they can find a power outlet.
They all climbed up the mountain, and now
    they have to climb down again.
The amazing machine says "hello" very quietly.

ACKNOWLEDGEMENTS

Some of these poems have been published before, sometimes in somewhat different versions, in *1cent*, *BafterC*, *Catalyst*, CRASH, *dig*, *Hardscrabble*, *industrial sabotage*, *Northern Testicle Review*, *Peter F. Yacht Club*, *Peter O'Toole*, *_Room to Move*, *Twaddle*, and *Unarmed*, on the Chaudiere Books blog, the Dusie Tuesday poem, and *The Week Shall Inherit the Verse*, in a red iron sheet, in the chapbooks *Mutations* (Book*hug), *Joyce's Walking Stick* (Double Negative), *Heart badly buried by five shovels* (Paper Kite Press), in the above/ground chapbooks *Opening the Dictionary*, *Albanian Suite*, and *Six Swedish Poets*, in the shreeking violet press chapbook *Eleven/Elleve/Alive*, in the anthology *Shift and Switch*, the Scream Festival anthology *Collected Works*, and in the Toronto Small Press Fair's instant anthologies *Prodigal Son of the Instant Anthology* and *Boogie Nights Instant Anthology*. Thanks to all those involved in these publications.

Thanks to Karen Mac Cormack for getting the ball rolling, to Erín Moure for encouragement, to Stuart Ross for a thorough pruning, to Leigh Nash and the team at Invisible Publishing for making it happen, and to Maria for being there.

Thanks to everyone whose words have nourished this book.

SOURCES

The Guitarist Federico Garcia Lorca, La Guitarra

Mutation Elizabeth Brandt, undergraduate biology essay

Roman Elegy Johann Wolfgang von Goethe, Römische Elegie III

Opening the Dictionary dictionaries (Swedish, French, Irish, German, Romanian, Japanese, Swedish)

Mirror-writing Korean text (no further details known)

Act of Thanking Erín Moure, glossary to Little Theatres

American Sonnet Nordstrom, girls' clothing department

Summer Georg Trakl, Sommer (faithful translation)

Unsigned City Italo Calvino, Le città invisibili, Le città e i segni, 4

Metropolitan Advertisements, Mexico City

Visible City Le Cento Grandi Città, Arnolodo Mondadori editore

Some Swedish Poets
  I: Eva-Stina Byggmästar, Älvdrottningen,
  "Schäslåååang..."
  II: Pernilla Berglund, Tilltar, "Se dig över fjället..."
  III: Eva-Stina Byggmästar, Älvdrottningen,
  "Myltasäck..."

Sappho XXXI Sappho, Fragment 31

We Get Lost Harry Martinson, Namnlöst

Safety Instructions from the seat pocket of a plane in
Japan

Juvenile Ode Tomas Tranströmer, Fem strofer till
Thoreau

Stars Edith Södergran, Stjärnorna (faithful translation)

The City Carlos Drummond de Andrade, Telegrama
de Moscou

Turkish Letter several poems from Pom^2

Exercise Anne Tardos, About the mechanism of
response writing, as for PomPom

Music I Heard with You Adam Zagajewski, Muzyka
słuchana z tobą

Self-portrait Unwilling to Sit Adam Zagajewski, Autoportret, nie wolny od wątpliwości

Epithalamion Adam Zagajewski, Epitalamium

Welcome Dutch/Japanese phrasebook

Night in a Coal Pit Harry Martinson, "Har ni sett en koltramp..."

Unofficial Translation Ecclesiastes 7:29, in French translation

He Said translations back into English of translations into Nynorsk by Dag Straumsvåg, of the following poems by Stuart Ross.
    I: Landscape
    II: Who knows?
    III: Road Trip, Southern Ontario, 1999
    IV: Bulletin
    V: Coffee Break
    VI: Survival
    VII: Three in a Room
    VIII: Poem

Early Rainer Maria Rilke, Früher Apollo

From the Time Jèssica Pujol Duran's Catalan translation of Sunday from Lisa Robertson's The Weather

Fresh Morning Willem Roggeman, Op een frisse morgen

Triumph Edith Södergran, Triumf att finnas till...

The Strange Mine of Pork Poetry
Portuguese translation of interview with Stuart Ross
by Dani Couture, Agulha 53

Twenty-three Plus Seven Psalm 23, King James Bible

Swedish Winter Tomas Tranströmer, Sex vintrar

Albanian Suite Visar Zhiti.
    I (unsure)
    II: Pazari i vjetër
    III: (unsure)
    IV: !
    V: Gjërat e vogla
    VI: Në detin e Homerit
    VII: Çastet ikin
    VIII: Dhe në Itali mund te qash; Koloseu

INVISIBLE PUBLISHING produces fine Canadian literature for those who enjoy such things. As an independent, not-for-profit publisher, our work includes building communities that sustain and encourage engaging, literary, and current writing.

Invisible Publishing has been in operation for over a decade. We released our first fiction titles in the spring of 2007, and our catalogue has come to include works of graphic fiction and non-fiction, pop culture biographies, experimental poetry, and prose.

We are committed to publishing diverse voices and experiences. In acknowledging historical and systemic barriers, and the limits of our existing catalogue, we strongly encourage LGBTQ2SIA+, Indigenous, and writers of colour to submit their work.

Invisible Publishing is also home to the Bibliophonic series of music books and the Throwback series of CanLit reissues.

If you'd like to know more please get in touch:
info@invisiblepublishing.com